WHY I LOVE GRANDMA

Other books by Gregory E. Lang:

Why a Daughter Needs a Dad

Why a Son Needs a Dad

Why I Love Grandpa

WHY I LOVE GRANDMA

100 reasons

GREGORY E. LANG

with Meagan Lang

Cumberland House
Nashville, Tennessee

Published by
  Cumberland House Publishing, Inc.
  431 Harding Industrial Drive
  Nashville, TN 37211

Cover design: Unlikely Suburban Design
Text design: Lisa Taylor

Library of Congress Cataloging-in-Publication Data

Lang, Gregory E., 1960–
    Why I love grandma: 100 reasons / Gregory E. Lang with Meagan Lang.
        p. cm.
    ISBN 1-58182-356-8
    1. Grandmothers—Miscellanea. 2. Grandparent and child—Miscellanea. I. Lang, Meagan, 1990– II. Title.
    HQ759.9.L343 2003b
    306.874'5—dc21

                                                                    2003012617

Printed in the United States of America
1 2 3 4 5 6 7 8 — 08 07 06 05 04 03

Dedicated with love to Gloria Dianne Lang and Ann Hord

and in memory of

Annie Ruth Lamberth Brown
and
Mary Myrtle Jacobs Lang

To Granna and MaMa for raising such
wonderful children who are now doing their best to do
the same for me. I love you both.

—Meagan

Introduction

Thanksgiving is a reunion holiday for my family. It is a time when three generations converge on one house to laugh, play, talk, sing, and share a few enormous meals together. Biscuits as big as your fist with butter and homemade preserves for breakfast, and turkey, ham, cornbread dressing, bowls and bowls of vegetables, and cakes and pies for dinner, all made from my beloved late grandmother's recipes, serve the seventy or so people who have come together to celebrate.

Sometime during the day the highly treasured family heirloom The Thanksgiving Book is brought out and shared, and the storytelling begins, reminding us all of why we have gathered together. An eight-inch-thick photo album, The Thanksgiving Book is filled with photographs of our family, all of which were taken at previous Thanksgiving celebrations. These pictures go back more than thirty years to the first Thanksgiving reunion that marked the beginnings of our tradition, the time we came together to comfort our grandfather and one another as we mourned the loss of my grandmother, Annie Ruth Lambert Brown, known to all as "Grandmomma."

Although there are members of my family who never met my grandmother, or were so young at the time of her loss that they have no memories to call upon, everyone knows who she was. Each of her four daughters resembles her in her own way, and their children in turn also carry features that someone can point to and say, "Those are Grandmomma's eyes," or "That's Grandmomma's smile." As the great grandchildren who never knew her savor the sweet taste of a dessert made from a recipe handed down over four generations, they are told about Grandmomma. As the newest cooks in the family learn to make cornbread dressing and giblet gravy from scratch, they hear of how

Grandmomma used to make it in the early morning, and of how the smell greeted all as they arrived at her house for a holiday meal.

Grandmomma was a short, plump woman with a face that always bore a smile. She wore horn-rimmed glasses and piled her silver hair high on her head, and nearly always had an apron tied around her waist. There were warm hugs upon greeting and departure, goodnight kisses for the lucky ones who got to spend the night, and a comforting hand on the shoulder of the one who walked next to her into church.

Grandmomma indulged her many grandchildren. I remember my cousin and me sitting at her feet, eating boiled peanuts she had just taken off the stove, as she watched the *Lawrence Welk Show*. Whether it was homemade peach ice cream, strawberry and rhubarb cobbler, or her famous Texas Pecan Cake, there was always a dessert in the house to look forward to after the dinner dishes were cleared from the table. On warm summer afternoons we sat on the front porch and shelled peas or shucked corn and listened to her as she told us about her early days, our grandfather, and our parents.

The first great loss my young heart experienced was on the evening I learned that Grandmomma had died. I was inconsolable and grieved her loss deeply, as did the rest of the family, especially my grandfather, who was never the same after that evening. Sometimes I look back and regret that I was so young at the time, too young to know then that time spent with someone you love is precious because that time is not guaranteed. Realizing this now, I make sure my daughter, Meagan Katherine, has ample opportunities to spend time with her extended family, especially her grandparents.

Meagan has loving and unique relationships with both of her grandmothers, known to her as "Granna" and "MaMa." Whether learning to quilt, playing rummy, watching old black and white movies, shopping, or making peppermint candy, my daughter loves the time she spends with her grandmothers. She understands that their influence in her life helps to shape her as she grows toward becoming a woman, when she will one day be a mother and then a grandmother and will in turn hand down traditions and delight the heart of a child as only a grandmother can. Once, as I watched my child learn from my mother how to make biscuits from scratch and listened as Mother told Meagan of how she learned this skill from her mother, I felt yet again the pain of my loss so many years ago and wished I could sit on the porch and reminisce with Grandmomma again.

My child loves her grandparents just as I loved mine and looks forward to the time she spends with them. She helped me write this book and its companion, *Why I Love Grandpa*, as a way to memorialize our love for those dear to us. Together we made a list of what each of us enjoyed about our grandmothers, and we thought of what we admired most about the many grandmother-grandchild relationships we observed during the photo shoots for this book.

With this book Meagan Katherine and I celebrate the grandmothers we love and recognize them for the many caring gestures they have extended to us. We also celebrate the wonderful grandmothers we met along the way, those who provide continuous and unselfish affection, who welcome new grandchildren into the family no matter what their origin, who soften the hard lessons of life, who remember their youth and relive it when given the chance to do so, and who speak with a wisdom and understanding that enrich the lives of those who listen. With this book we hope to give grandchildren a special way to reach out to their grandmothers and speak to them of what is in their hearts. The last spread of this book allows space for the grandchild to include a family photo and write his or her own one-hundredth reason for loving Grandma.

With each year something about our Thanksgiving tradition changes just a little. Those who were once children make the right of passage and move to sit at the adult tables. A new leader emerges within the youngest generation and rallies the cousins together in mischief. A son now helps the father; a daughter now hustles in the kitchen while the mother rests. A grandfather, the religious beacon in the family, passes the torch to a grandson who offers a prayer before eating. As we witness these changes take place, these signs that our family is ever evolving, someone inevitably says, "I wish Grandmomma could be here to see this." We mean this, of course, in the temporal sense, because we know that she *is* still with us—in our hearts, every day.

WHY I LOVE GRANDMA

I love Grandma because

she shows me that an old dog

can learn new tricks.

I love Grandma because

her faith in me gives me confidence.

I love Grandma because

she never lets me down.

I love Grandma because . . .

she lets me sleep as late as I want.

she keeps a pantry shelf stocked just for me.

she sends me gifts for no reason.

she makes divinity, just the way I like it,

every Christmas.

I love Grandma because

she has shown me that there is indeed lasting love.

I love Grandma because

she loves each of her grandchildren equally.

I love Grandma because . . .

she helps me plan for my future.

she brings me milk and cookies when I am sick.

she helps me understand my parents.

she remembers what others have long forgotten.

I love Grandma because

she talks to me like I'm an adult.

I love Grandma because

she has more energy than I do.

I love Grandma because . . .

she will watch reruns with me,
over and over again.

she doesn't care if I sing off-key.

she always carries a picture of me.

she can shop for hours.

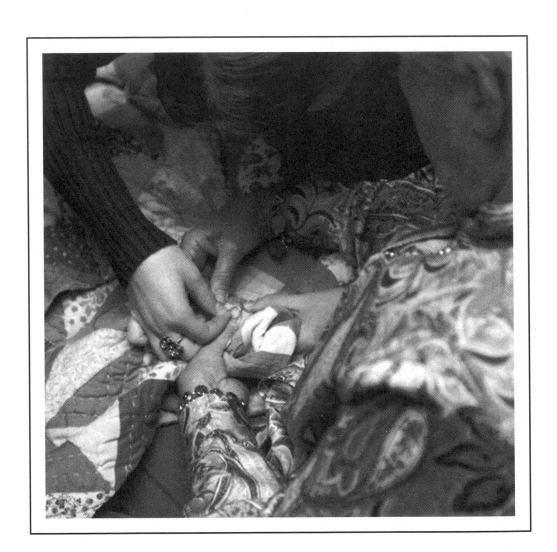

I love Grandma because

she teaches me how to do things

the old-fashioned way.

I love Grandma because

she can always turn a frown into a smile.

I love Grandma because

she teaches me to hold my arms open wide,

unless someone stands between them.

I love Grandma because

she lets me jump on the bed.

I love Grandma because . . .

she sends me cards to remind me
that she loves me.

she sings to me when I am blue.

she gives affection no matter who is watching.

she still believes in Santa Claus.

I love Grandma because

she is the first one to show up for everything I do.

I love Grandma because

she encourages me to be comfortable with who I am.

I love Grandma because

she doesn't care if I eat dessert before dinner.

I love Grandma because . . .

she falls asleep with me on the couch.

she smiles and waves to strangers.

she teaches me how to set a table.

she brushes away my tears with tenderness.

I love Grandma because

she takes time to let me learn at my own pace.

I love Grandma because . . .

she teaches me how to turn cartwheels.

she tells me to kiss someone every day.

she shows me how to make paper dolls.

she makes chocolate-chip pancakes.

I love Grandma because

she can still see rabbits and giraffes in the clouds.

I love Grandma because

she teaches me to love nature.

I love Grandma because

she can be trusted to keep secrets.

I love Grandma because

she teaches me to be grateful for what I have.

I love Grandma because

she brags about me all the time.

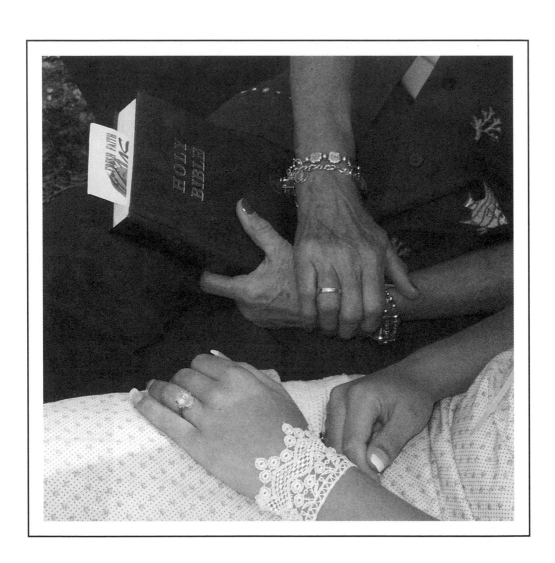

I love Grandma because

she loves the fellowship of her church.

～

I love Grandma because . . .

she never discourages me from asking questions.

she doesn't care how many friends show up

with me when I come to visit.

she lends a hand when my parents need help.

she keeps a spare bedroom prepared for me.

I love Grandma because

she saves things she knows will be

of interest to me one day.

I love Grandma because

she encourages me to use my imagination.

I love Grandma because

she shares with me what took her

years to learn.

I love Grandma because

she knows when not to take me seriously.

I love Grandma because . . .

she never thinks I'm too old to be spoiled.

she teaches me that it is wise to seek advice.

she helps me learn from my mistakes.

she shows me that change is good.

I love Grandma because

she has more patience with me than anyone else does.

I love Grandma because

she teaches me how to bake.

I love Grandma because

she always says the right thing at the right time.

I love Grandma because

I see myself in her.

I love Grandma because . . .

she teaches me to enjoy getting my hands dirty.

she encourages an appreciation of the arts.

she teaches me to serve others.

she teaches me the virtue of being kind.

I love Grandma because

she is the glue that holds the family together.

I love Grandma because

she does not think I ask too much of her.

I love Grandma because . . .

she teaches me how to be a gracious host.

she passes down her secret family recipes to me.

she teaches me to honor my mate.

she shows me how to handle the
demands of a family.

I love Grandma because

she decorates with my artwork.

I love Grandma because

she doesn't mind that I am somewhat different.

I love Grandma because

she still calls me "precious."

I love Grandma because

she makes each grandchild feel uniquely special.

I love Grandma because . . .

she lets me wear her old jewelry.

she covers her refrigerator with pictures of me.

she always tucks me in and kisses me goodnight.

she leaves surprises under my pillow.

I love Grandma because

she can dance to my music.

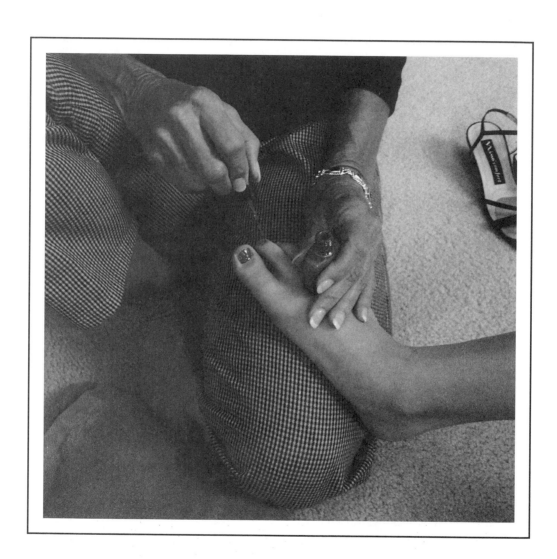

I love Grandma because

she teaches me to appreciate the significance

of small but sincere gestures.

I love Grandma because . . .

she teaches me to find the intrinsic value in everyone.

she doesn't expect too much from me.

she shares her favorite memories with me.

she reminds me not to forget those who have
helped me get to where I am.

I love Grandma because

she steers me away from the wrong friends.

I love Grandma because

she cooks my favorite foods.

I love Grandma because

she helps me to get beyond painful experiences.

I love Grandma because

she always thinks of others before herself.

I love Grandma because

she can make any day a special one for me.

I love Grandma because . . .

she is a safe spot for me to turn to.

she teaches me how to say grace.

she helps me do my hair.

she is always ready to hold my hand.

I love Grandma because . . .

she instinctively knows when I need a hug.

she teaches me how to be gracious.

she protects me from thunderstorms.

she knows how to host great tea parties.

I love Grandma because

without her my life would be less joyful.

Paste your picture here,
and write your reason
on the opposite page.

I love Grandma because

_____

Acknowledgments

This book could not have been written without the support and generosity of many people. I offer a special thanks to the families who shared their stories with me, who stood in the cold and wet to pose for these photographs, and who indulged me over and over again as I said, "Just one more." Meagan and I were touched by the love we witnessed in the time we spent with you.

I also wish to thank my friend Janet Lankford-Moran, who helped me hide my mistakes and gave me council while I pretended to be a photographer, and the administration of Greater Atlanta Christian school, which helped me recruit families to participate in creating this book.

Finally, I wish to thank Ron Pitkin and his staff at Cumberland House, who have encouraged me and helped me as I worked on this book. Ron, I appreciate your vision and thank you for giving me the venue to touch readers in the way that the books we have done together have. My deepest appreciation and warmest regards always.

TO CONTACT THE AUTHORS

write in care of the publisher:
Cumberland House Publishing
431 Harding Industrial Drive
Nashville, TN 37211

or email:
greg.lang@mindspring.com